Bring The Kids, Leave The Headache

by Hope Oriabure-Hunter

BRING THE KIDS
leave THE HEADACHE

by Hope Oriabure-Hunter

A COMPREHENSIVE GUIDE FOR BRINGING KIDS TO
GROWN-UP EVENTS

To request permissions, contact the author at

hopeo.king@outlook.com

Paperback ISBN: 978-1-952313-06-6

Ebook ISBN: 978-1-952313-07-3

Printed in the United States of America

Edited by Danielle Radden

Cover Art by Erin Funes

Layout by Danielle Radden

Confidence Lessons Publishing

www.ConfidenceLessonsPublishing.com

Dedication

This book is dedicated to my mother, Theresa Oriabure. She taught me how to be a mother.

When I was a newborn premature baby in 1978, I slept next to her with her hand on my chest to make sure my heart didn't stop beating in the night. This was before baby monitors were a normal consumer product. When I had my first baby, she drove over an hour in rush-hour traffic to be there. She missed my first son's birth by 10 minutes. I gave her a redo with my fourth and final child.

When I was getting ready to leave the hospital with my first born filled with anxiety and dealing with the physical shock of having a baby, she called me. She was on her way and I wasn't to touch anything once I got home. She would be there to help me.

Then when I had my fourth baby, she moved in with me for three months to help me. I told her I would be okay; I had this parent thing figured out. She is a mother of four herself, and told me it would be different. She was right. For all these times I have appreciated my mother for her help and sacrifices. But as I get older, I realize all the things she did for me I didn't know about or that I sophomorically brushed off mattered too. Mommy, I hope this book makes you proud.

Table of Contents

viii   *Preface*

1   Introduction

6   Introduction to Parties and Special
           Occasions

7   House Parties

13   Networking Events

20   Networking Play Date Partnership

24   Tailgate Parties

29   Parking Lot Tailgate Parties

33   Corporate Parties (Holiday)

41   Corporate Parties (Spring/Summer)

47   Church

50   Weddings

66   To Be Continued...

68   *Appendices*

Preface

It's never ideal to be a parent with the kids in tow at adult social events or special occasions. It is even less ideal for parents to be left out, isolated, and forgotten. But parents need more than a diaper bag packed to the gills and advanced behavior negotiations before heading to parties with their younger kids. These lonely mothers and fathers need solutions so that they don't have to sacrifice all semblance of a social life just because they have little ones. And that is why I have decided to write this guide for parents, planners, and event hosts who need to know how to plan for any event's littlest guests.

I own a special occasions event babysitting company, but more importantly, I am a parent who once tried to give up my social life and suffered because of it. I have first-hand knowledge of the risks involved with taking my kids to any event. I also have some proven strategies to mitigate those risks. I love being a Mommy. It's an unmatched, indescribable gift, but it can be extremely isolating without some social outings. By writing this guide, I hope to make "partying" with little people easier. Bring the kids, and leave the headache.

BRING THE KIDS
Leave THE HEADACHE

Introduction

Coming Out Party

I separated from my children's father while I was pregnant with my last child. I was a single parent of four in a matter of months. Right on the heels of my delivery was my sister's wedding. I still don't know how I managed to get all four children dressed (ages 8-years, 6-years, 3-years, and 10-months). I even managed to get several cases of alcohol to my sister's venue. At the wedding, we had event sitting (we will get to that story later), and there were plenty of hands willing to hold my kids. My daughter and son had been the flower girl and ring bearer. My baby and toddler were undeniably cute in their suits. I felt included and supported. The wedding had set a standard for what could be possible.

The situation, while ideal, was an anomaly. For most of the time my children were little, I was side-lined with my kids. My mother warned me, "It wouldn't be 'right' for me to bring my kids, not even to family occasions." So for almost two years I sat at home, struggling with isolation and detachment. Roughly 90% of mothers feel especially lonely during the first few years of their child's life, and that can be especially problematic for single parents. Staying at home might be easier, but it's not always the best choice for mental health.

Finally, I said enough. My cousin was having a birthday party at his home and invited me *and the kids*. I decided to go despite my mother's reservations. I got the children all ready, packed the diaper bag, and we were off. We listened to music in the car, and everyone was happy and glad to be on an outing. When we arrived, I was greeted by my cousin's wife and surprised expressions from several of the guests. They hadn't seen me in years, yet here I was trying to get my gaggle of kids through the door. The space was narrow, so my kids linked hands and wove through an obstacle course of people, furniture, and food, searching for my parents. Before we could find our target, my littlest boy had spotted a box of cereal on top of the fridge. He loved cereal—**loved** it. Immediately he began to buck out of my arms and cry. My father whisked him away and tried to calm him down. The reverse happened though— my son cried so loudly he caught the attention of all the guests. But this wasn't the worst embarrassment to come. I took my sobbing child from my Dad and moved to another room with less people. He didn't calm down, so my cousin's wife brought him the box of cereal and he began to eat. Within seconds he started to vomit all over me and himself. I was so embarrassed, and for a second my embarrassment took precedence over making sure he was okay. My cousin's wife quickly brought me a towel and assured me everything was fine. My Dad's facial expression said it all though. It was time to leave. Despite my cousin's wife's insistence, I got my kids together and managed to get to the car with a vomit-soaked dress, and a heavy heart of regret and disappointment.

Why had I tried to go to this event? What was I thinking? What could I have done differently, if anything? Could my cousin have hidden the box of cereal? Was I destined to stay at home, alone?

About This Guide

I was left to ponder these questions with no real answers, so I continued to stay home for several more years except for selective occasions. But I **have** answers now, and you don't have to stay home feeling isolated and stuck like I did. In this guide you will get advice that is based on specific occasions, with preparation instructions for parents, and tips for event hosts and planners.

There are a few assumptions.

> 1.   This advice is best for parents of babies, toddlers, and preschoolers.

> 2.   The information is geared toward parents of children who are "typically developing." In the appendix we will address special needs kids—I have a son on the spectrum too.

> 3.   This guide should be read in advance. Don't try to crack this book open on the ride to the event. The top strategy for attending events successfully with your little ones is to plan appropriately.

This book is **not** meant to be read from cover to cover; rather choose the event(s) you plan to attend, then read the appropriate section. Each section stands on its own, but you may see some reoccurring advice because it makes sense (the one-gallon freezer bag is a favorite!) The book looks to move past obvious and predictable advice (pack a diaper bag). Rather it aims to give practical and insightful advice and suggestions that you can use with confidence. Everything may not apply to you, but at least read it. It could be information you pass around to your circle of friends or family.

There are no paid advertisements or sponsored content. If I mentioned a product, brand, place, or person, it's because I love and endorse it.

Introduction to Parties and Special Occasions

People need parties and special occasions. Research indicates that social interactions are a major buffer of depression and improves a person's general well-being. Most of the time parties are welcoming events. They can offer a great opportunity to develop friendships or they can be a real confidence builder (like attending your first middle school party). Special occasions can help people bond and build community like at engagement parties or repass gatherings. At parties you can gain acceptance—you were invited after all. You don't have to throw away all these good party benefits just because you are a parent.

We will start with "House Parties" because that is where my party debacle started.

House Parties

I know it's hard to forget the images of Kid 'n Play, the popular hip-hop duo who starred in and produced the 1990s series of hysterical "House Party" films. But for our purposes we are defining a house party as a type of party with a medium to large group of people gathered at the personal residence of the host. People have house parties for a range of reasons from house blessings to "we haven't seen each other in a while."

Parent Preparation

Establish the purpose of the party. Is it a celebration you were personally invited to, and will the host would be disappointed if you don't show up? Or is it a party where a large net was cast on a Facebook group invite? Do you really need to go? The reason why I ask is because between the day your child is born, and the time they turn 18, you get 940 Saturdays with them, and 260 of those days are gone by your child's fifth birthday. Use your time with your kids wisely.

Choose your ensemble carefully. A small detail I left out of my house party horror story was that I wore a dress with a plunging neckline. I wanted to show I still had it. It was impossible to not flash people with my son clinching onto it during his tantrum. And let me just say I had vomit in my bra. Be cute, but still wear clothes that will allow you to complete your parent duties (bending, picking-up, and assisting little people).

This may be sophomoric to mention, but **bring yourself a change of clothes.** Perhaps if I had brought a change of clothes, I would have been able to change at the party and stay. Just like for yourself, I recommend that you bring a change of clothes for your kids (yes even potty-trained ones). They are in a new environment and may not make it to the bathroom in time, or they may

8

not feel comfortable telling you they have to go. Bring two gallon-size freezer bags so you don't get caught in the bathroom washing everything out. With the freezer bags, you can quickly address the issue and get back to the party. Worry when you get home about washing dirty clothes, or just throwing them away—don't act like you don't tango with this idea.

Find out what to bring. House parties are more casual affairs, and may be a potluck; the host provides the meat and the guests bring the sides and sweets. Call ahead and volunteer for something quick (prepackaged is even better). You will surely have plenty of pre-work before attending the party with getting the kid(s) ready, packing their stuff, and getting yourself ready. You do not want to complicate things by having to "cook" too.

Arrive on time or early. This way you can review the party landscape and lay claim to your space. Maybe that means finding a comfortable armchair with a small free space next to it where your child can play closely. Also, arriving early can give you a chance to find out where the bathrooms are, and ask about access to a spare bedroom or living room to change a baby.

Host Tips:

Confirm your RSVPs for guests with kids. Call these guests to let them know how many kids you anticipate coming and their ages. Parents may choose not to bring their child if no one else is bringing kids. or if all the other children guests are older.

Have a kid's space. Never assume a parent will not come with their child if children were welcomed in the initial invite. Always plan as if they are coming. Allocate a space where parents can mingle with parents, and kids with kids (a second living room or eat-in kitchen if available), but don't necessarily segregate them. If you don't have a separate space, try to keep food trays and snacks at a higher level to prevent little hands from getting all over your carefully composed charcuterie.

When preparing for the party get low (not a refence to the popular club anthem by Ying Yang Twins). Get on your knees, so you can see what your littlest guest sees. You would hate for them to grab precious figurines off a shelf because you hadn't thought of them being in their reach.

Stow garbage cans in the bottom of cabinets or other inconspicuous places in both the bathroom and kitchen (a practical but seldom said tip). Little people sometimes do not understand that perfectly edible food cannot be eaten once discarded into the trash. And you do not want them dumpster diving in the bathroom trash, which may have disposable razors or other dangerous trash. Also put toxic items like cleaners, toiletries, and medicines out of reach.

House Parties

Event Planner Tips:

If you have been hired to plan and execute a large house party, don't forget to plan for kids just like your adult guests. If you are going to have a catered meal, put some consideration into what the children will eat. Parents may take offense if you have a great meal for the adults and Lunchables for their kids. In fact, in a worst-case scenario you may have parents who feed their children off the adult buffet because they feel the children's food is inadequate, thus skewing your meal count and potentially causing you to run out of food.

Understand media rooms are not babysitters. Do not plan for kids to be kept in a media room with movies all evening—it's not enough. They still require supervision, not to mention the average media room starts at $16,000, which raises the stakes even more. There are a lot of expensive electronics that little hands could easily break. Additionally, kids left unsupervised may be tempted to make on-demand purchases without permission. You will want to supervise the adults who have access to the children too. A child predator might pay special attention to a child and make him or her feel special. They typically get to know the child's likes and dislikes very well, and knowing favorite movie titles could be the start.

Networking Events

Networking has become a vital catalyst for every type of business, whether fortune 1,000, small, or multi-level marketing. Networking is an opportunity to form relationships with others and expand your business. Why should parents miss out on being business leaders and finding customers, partners, and opportunities for growth? They shouldn't. But I will not lie, this can be tricky. Typically, in my experience, networking events happen early in the morning, the early evening, or during the lunch hour. Well, the extended lunch hour because they are usually from 11:30 AM to 1:00 PM. These are tough times to attend events if you are a stay-at-home parent, or the time doesn't jive with your Mother's Day out program hours.

My event sitting company has tried arduously for years to partner with networking groups and associations to provide pop-up childcare during these events. We advocate that childcare is as much of an investment as food or drinks—childcare increases participation and reduces stress for the attendees. Still no taco. We have had one consistent networking group client (we will talk about that success in a moment).

We found that most millennials run the "hip" networking groups and don't believe there is a need for childcare. One such millennial told me, "Nobody will want to worry about their child in the next room while they have a mid-afternoon or an evening drink with a potential connection." The only way we can change this narrative is for Mompreneurs, Dadprenuers, Grannyprenuers, and Papapreneurs to ask for this service. And for our allies to support us by advocating until childcare is as commonplace at networking events as bottled water, pens, and notepads! Okay, off my soapbox and onto advice.

Parent Preparation

Establish the purpose for your attendance. Before you go to any networking event, you need to be clear on what you would like to accomplish by attending the event. Is it being hosted by an association you are considering joining? Are there connections you want to make that are visible on the RSVP list? Is the keynote speaker somebody who inspires you? As parents, sometimes we must balance doing something to "keep up with the Jones's" verses doing what makes sense for our families. In the event/wedding industry, networking can be very social. Several of these events take place in the evening at venues with tremendous food, décor, and music, showcasing industry best. Sometimes seeing industry friends post on social media and living their best lives, I get jealous. But when my ten-year-old is reading to me, snuggled under my arm, I know I have made the right decision to give my attention to my kids in the evenings.

Contact the event organizer. If childcare is not advertised as provided at a networking event you are considering, call the organizer to ask. Do not assume it will be okay to bring your child. Even an event that seems child-friendly, might not be prepared for little ones. A few weeks ago, I attended an excellent Mompreneurs mastermind event with a wonderful panel and an incredible keynote speech about balancing careers and motherhood. To my surprise they did not offer childcare.

A single mother came, wearing her baby in a carrier. The baby was very quiet, and often her mother stood with her, swaying side to side. It was refreshing to hear the baby cooing amongst the sound advice and transparency from the panel and the speaker. But what if the baby had cried and been a distraction, and the mother had been asked to leave? What if she had been stopped at the door and was unable to attend at all?

If childcare is offered, keep your cellphone where it will get your attention if needed. We provided childcare at a come-and-go networking event that offered vendor tables to businesses in addition to the networking. Parents could come with their children and drop them off in our separate care room for a block of time. We made sure we provided parents with our nursery pagers in case their child needed them. We did not want to have to go into the exhibition area and start hunting down a parent who was making meaningful business connections. If your event childcare provider doesn't provide pagers, be sure to have your phone on vibrate or have a special ringtone so you can be alerted. Networking can be loud with so many conversations going on and the occasional background music. It will be comforting for you to know you can be reached if you are needed, even in a loud space.

Make sure your child has eaten and the networking event isn't disrupting their sleeping routine. Your children may not be happy to be in a new place and away from you, so don't complicate things by neglecting food or having them over-tired.

Search networking groups' event calendars for family-friendly events. Several networking groups have annual family-friendly events where networkers are encouraged to bring their family.

Host Tips:

Poll attendees four to six months in advance for major networking events to see if they would be interested in childcare during the event. If so, this gives you time to advertise properly and set up a registration system.

Consider hiring a professional event sitting service, because volunteers may not have experience with children guests. Or your attendees may have a less-than-ideal experience with a potential connection's child, which could threaten future business for both individuals.

Event Planner Tips:

When looking for a venue for major networking events, **consider the requirements for a potential childcare room** when conducting your site visit. If you don't know what to look for, you can contact me for a checklist.

If creating a family-friendly networking event, pair it with a national holiday (i.e. Christmas, Easter, or Spring Break). Parent's will be more enthusiastic to come if they don't have to take the kids out of school.

When creating a family-friendly networking event, don't be afraid to "break the script." The Chic Network, a Dallas, TX based networking group of event and wedding industry professionals typically meets at upscale hotels and event venues in the evening. For its family-friendly networking event they met at the famed Dallas World Aquarium in the early afternoon and it was a hit!

Networking Events

Networking Play Date Partnership

One day while on Facebook, I saw an upcoming event for a *Networking Play Date*. I was intrigued and my calendar was open, so I decided to go. I had no idea how much that decision would change my life. The tribe of women I met there have become some of my biggest cheerleaders.

Networking Play Date is the brainchild of Sara Belmonte. Sara is the owner of Design Remodel Pros, a custom design remodeling company. She founded Moms Out Marketing (MOM) to support moms in their journey through mommy-hood and provide a framework to help others grow. But the remarkable thing about Sara was she had the forward thinking to provide networking opportunities where children were welcomed. Not even the Mompreneurs mastermind had thought this way.

The networking offered wasn't designed as a family-friendly event with a child-focused activity or carnival atmosphere either. This was true networking with 30-second introductions, a speaker, and light refreshments. The only difference was that it took place in a yogurt joint, and the kids could mill around happily in the indoor play area or dangle from their mother's legs as we sat. It sounds like chaos, but it wasn't, nor has it ever been. With moms on the ready to hold kids, each mommy could introduce herself without losing a beat. Women who ordinarily could not network are present, learning, connecting, and growing their businesses. After a one-on-one with Sara, I decided my event sitting company would support the networking event with a sitter. Our sitter would be able to help with the younger kids and provide more structured activities. Guess what happened? It made a good thing better. In hopes you are part of an extraordinary networking opportunity like this one, I have just one parent preparation and one tip for an event host.

Networking Play Date Partnership

Parent preparation:

With networking where your child is free to roam—
either close to you or with other play opportunities—**let
the helpers know if your child has separation anxiety**.
Setting realistic expectations will alleviate some of your
anxiety while networking. It's important for event sitters
to make your child feel comfortable and acclimated.
The sitters who work with me are always disappointed
in the few instances when a child just couldn't be left in
our care. If we know the child has separation anxiety,
then we don't take it personally, and will bring them
promptly back to the mom, because we had already
gotten permission to do so.

Host/Planner:

Please **poll your attendees** and see how many networkers have young children and would appreciate a childcare service. Don't be afraid to challenge the status quo. To quote David Ogilvy, "In the modern world of business, it is useless to be a creative, original thinker unless you also sell what you create."

Networking Play Date Partnership

Tailgate Parties

Football in Texas is just about as big as the state itself. Friday nights are reserved for high school football, whether your child is on the field or not. Saturday nights may be college football, then on Sundays, Texas households host America's team, the Dallas Cowboys. So being invited to a tailgate party in some form or fashion is inevitable here.

For the purpose of this guide we will discuss two types of tailgate parties: the party that takes place in a home (variation of a house party), and the tailgate party that takes place in a parking lot.

We will tackle the *home* tailgate party first.

Parent Preparation

Establish your purpose for attendance. Tailgating parties can be a lot of fun—adult fun that is. There can be drinking, heated team rivalries amongst guests, and foul language. When deciding to attend this type of party, consider the other invited guests and their temperament. Is this a group that would be fun and mindful that kids are around? Or is this a group that, after a couple of drinks, would have escalating unruly behavior? If it's the latter, skip this party because of the unstable atmosphere.

For your 3 and 4-year-olds, consider bringing a tablet. This is one of the only times I would recommend technology. I don't generally believe childcare or child-minding should be subsidized with technology. But if everyone's attention is on a tv screen, theirs will be too. They might not understand why they can't watch *PJ Masks* or *Paw Patrol* on the big screen, because you usually concede at home.

Make and take an activity bag. Fill the bag with non-interruptive toys, games, books, or activities that can be brought out during the game. Also include noise-cancelling headphones, because a sudden victorious cheer could startle young kids.

Bring healthy snack alternatives for your kids. As adults, we reserve this type of occasion to gorge on unhealthy eats and snack foods. But for little ones, having so many snacks in endless proportions may be overwhelming. You don't want to have the conversation why they can't eat the entire bowl of chips—because we need to leave some for others, it's not healthy to eat so many chips…yada, yada, yada. Instead, bring baggies of frozen grapes, squeeze yogurt pouches, and fruit bars.

Tailgate Parties

Host Tips:

Plan for the kids to be amid the action. My event sitting company has been booked to watch children at large home tailgate parties. We are always glad when hosts take time to consider their littlest guests. But don't think that if you put a bounce house in the backyard, the kids will want to be there the entire time, even with supervision.

For example, one of our clients had planned for us to be in the backyard for most of the event with her children guests. But she hadn't considered that it would be getting dark before half-time. Luckily, the house had a converted garage that we could use for mealtime. Ahead of time we had arranged child-sized chairs and folding tables, so we were able to move their activities indoors, and of course we had board games in the car.

Planner Tips:

If planning activities for children guests, stage at least two areas. The children will get bored easily if they must stay in one place for the duration of the party. The children can be moved to the second area during half-time.

Consider serving mocktails. These drinks can be offered to designated drivers, pregnant women, party guests who choose not to drink, and children. You will have to worry less about ill-fated taste-testing of alcoholic beverages, because children mistook a beer can for a soda.

Parking Lot Tailgate Parties

This type of tailgating party occurs in the parking lots of stadiums and arenas before (and occasionally after) games and concerts. This involves several other people you don't know, opposed to the house tailgating party, but can be a once in a lifetime experience. At AT&T Stadium, the home of the Dallas Cowboys, it's quite the spectacle. The stadium has fifteen parking lots with designated tailgating spaces located around the perimeter of each lot.

Parent Preparation

Establish your purpose for attendance. No caution content here. I would want to go if offered!

Don't come early. Parking lot tailgating takes preparation. Let your tailgate host set up without the distraction of littles. The parking lots typically open five hours before the game, so arriving after the first two hours gives you plenty of time to enjoy the experience, but gives your host plenty of time to prepare. In fact, if your host is just tailgating and not attending the game, AT&T Stadium lets you keep tailgating for two hours after the game ends. So you potentially have an entire day to be there.

Bring a small set of plastic shelves. You can use these to set up an easily accessible small command center. It's better than constantly rifling through a diaper bag for essentials like sunscreen and bottles. You will also want to bring a first aid kit—something you typically wouldn't bring to a party. You will be outside, in the elements, in a parking lot, so bandages for falls on concrete and medicine to treat bug stings are helpful.

Make an ID bracelet for your child. Include your name, phone number, and information that can identify where you are located. For example, at AT&T Stadium, I would write the parking lot number. If your child is lost, someone helping them can start making their way to you as they try to reach you on your phone.

If you plan on attending the game, most stadiums can provide ID bracelets at their fan accommodation or guest services centers. In case your child is lost, check-in with the nearest event staff member. Look up the guest services hotline and save the number into your phone **before** you arrive at the stadium.

⊗

Bring food and snacks for your littles. One of the crown jewels of tailgating is grilling. Your kids may not appreciate hot dogs with the "black-of-the grill" on them. Pre-boil hot dogs, and then use the buns and other condiments from your host. For babies who are less discerning about how food looks, they can eat food off the grill at around six-months-old.

⊗

Determine the stroller policy for the stadium. While tailgating, it's advisable to bring a large stroller that can hold your child and double as a mobile nursery. If you plan to stay for the game, most stadiums favor the little umbrella strollers and may require that the large stroller be checked-in at a guest services center.

⊗

Parking Lot Tailgate Parties

One-gallon freezer bag. If you plan on attending the game, the NFL and other professional and collegiate leagues have bag policies. They strongly encourage fans to limit the number of items brought with them into the stadium. You can carry a clear tote with specified measurements or just use a one-gallon freezer bag.

Parking Lot Tailgate Parties

Corporate Parties (Holiday)

Gone are the days of the 9-to-5 holiday party hosted at the office. Remember the potluck menus, the round of white-elephant gifts, and the awkwardness of having to socialize with co-workers you never speak to except for an occasional "hello" in passing? Today companies make big productions of holiday parties. These parties can build company culture, boost employee morale, and (for our purposes) make framed family pictures come to life.

There isn't anything as whimsical as a child's excitement during the holidays. These corporate parties often try to capture this magic by having children-inspired activities or installations as a cornerstone of the event (Santa for example).

Corporate Parties (Holiday)

Parent Preparation

Establish the purpose of your attendance. Well, if it's your job you must go, and if it's your spouse's job you must go. Simply put, although it's a party for company employees, employees see each other all day, every day. They are coming to the party to see significant others.

Choose your ensemble carefully. According to InStyle magazine, among all the holiday festivities, "the company party ensemble is arguably the most important." No pressure or anything. Well, from a Mommy prospective, I always tried to have my kids in matching clothes and colors when it came to special occasions. Typically at these events, there are family photo opportunities to take advantage of. But don't beat yourself up trying to find the perfect set of outfits for the family to wear. The most important thing is that your family looks clean and nice.

Corporate Parties (Holiday)

Find out what special activities they have planned for the children guests ahead of time. This way you can plan what activities your children will participate in and which ones you may choose to avoid. For example, I am not a fan of face painting at formal events. Don't get me wrong, with my event babysitting company we work with an incredible face painter—it's just the picture thing. I'm not sure I want my child to have a stocking on the side of her face in our company-provided family picture.

Get the ChangerClutch. In this guide, I have tried to stay clear of making specific service and product suggestions. This book is to help parents, not sell to them. But the ChangerClutch is an outstanding product. Bringing a diaper bag may be hard if the children are mixing with the adults and there is not a dedicated area for kids and their stuff. The ChangerClutch is a stylish streamline clutch that converts to a changing pad and can hold diapers. I know! Find more information in the appendix.

Find out if the event will host a quiet room with sleeping solutions. For events that run past 10:00 PM, I always suggest sleeping solutions (i.e. cots, play-yards, or portable bassinets). If your event host is not going to provide a quiet room, you may need to make plans to leave early, or have a friend or family member pick-up the kids from the party. Soliciting help to watch sleeping kids can't be that bad—right?

Monitor your drinking. My event babysitting company never wishes to release a child to overly intoxicated parents. We work with the event host and the planner to determine the best way to get both the parent and child home safely.

However, also consider the next day. A report out of the University of Michigan found that a quarter of the 1,200 parents polled admitted that they freely indulged at holiday parties and other special events, even though they knew they had to take care of their kids as soon as they left. Although they made it home safely, these inebriated moms and dads said they tended to just hope for the best when it came to getting the kids to bed and to having a calm, hangover free morning.

Be mindful of introducing co-workers to your kids. Keep in mind little ones do not understand the significance of titles, or social graces. Do not expect your kids to be cute on cue. To make the process easier, try to make introductions while your child is content. Also do not pull them away from activities they are enjoying which may cause them to express confused, angry, or sad emotions. Establish boundaries for people holding and touching your kids; you do not want to put your child in uncomfortable physical situations.

Corporate Parties (Holiday)

Host Tip:

Poll your employees to see if event babysitting is needed. I stumbled across an article entitled "10 Reasons Why Employees Loathe Company Holiday Parties." You guessed it, number three on the list was finding babysitters. Yet the article's author Suzanne Lucas asserted that children at a company party is a can't-win situation. She cautioned, "...if you invite children, the holiday party can quickly turn into a kid's party. This is fine if the staff is comprised of families, but is likely to leave your childless employees feeling like they aren't even a guest at the party. Parents don't want to deal with the hassle of babysitters, but they can't bring the kids."

What to do? My event babysitting company is not a referee in the scenario, but we do believe our services are a win-win for both parent and non-parents. It is up to the host to find out what will work best for the most attendees.

We have provided care at corporate holiday parties for years, and have always been welcomed by parents. In fact, non-parents have been complimentary of our services as well.

Planner Tips:

When planning activities for children guests, be mindful of their ages and dress. We once had a corporate holiday party client who booked cookie decorating, but over 25% of their children guests were toddlers or younger. These children were much too young to participate or appreciate the activity. Also (soapbox moment) I don't like face painters at formal events where families have opportunities to take pictures with Santa or in front of festive backdrops.

Do not give wrapped gifts to children guests. The experience is gift enough. We have a corporate client that gives its children guests gifts upon arrival at their event. The children are encouraged to open them immediately. This causes immense logistical pains for my team, as we must deal with missing toy pieces and yards of wrapping paper trash. If anything, give the gifts at the end of the night, then let the parents handle it.

Consider setting up a quiet room. This room can be multi-purpose and serve different guest needs. It could be a mothering room for nursing mothers, or a safe place for children with sensory sensitivities. You could set up sleeping solutions for younger children, so their parents can enjoy the evening. If your event is in a hotel,

Corporate Parties (Holiday)

they typical have play-yards available, and you can rent cots for older kids. This room would need an attendant.

Hire a professional event sitting service. My company is full service as are most other event childcare providers. In addition to our sitters, we provide games, activities, and toys with sleeping and eating solutions (i.e. highchairs and booster seats) available for rent. Not only can our sitters create a separate event for children guests, we manage the moments that create their experience, including sleeping.

Corporate Parties (Holiday)

Corporate Parties (Spring/Summer)

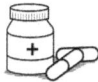

When I think of corporate spring or summer parties, it invokes images of Skyline Ranch—a family-owned Dallas staple with more than 25 years of business. To their guests they offer multiple sport courts, a swimming pool, pavilion, and a list of nostalgic outdoor games run by staff. All this on 90 acres with an incredible view of downtown Dallas. While companies have these events for the same reason as the holiday parties, the warmer weather presents its own challenges and preparation needs.

Parent Preparation:

Establish the purpose of your attendance. Did you skip the holiday party in favor of the casual, more playful environment of the spring/summer corporate party? Did this fit more into your schedule then during the holiday season? Whatever your reason, this occasion is one of the few in our list where children guests are typically planned for and expected.

Plan for your child's heat tolerance. This past summer I enrolled my children at our local YMCA summer camp. I anxiously attended our parent meeting. I always like to see how other child-inspired businesses operate. As they discussed the children's daily schedule and explained that there would be a lot of time spent outside, a parent's hand shot up. She exclaimed, "My son doesn't like being outside in the heat." I wanted to tell her, "Ma'am we are in Texas, you may need to enroll your child in a different camp." The reality is that if your kids doesn't like being hot, you may need to pass on this event altogether. Little ones can't always express their discomfort in words and may just have a temper tantrum. In the summer, the sun is at its strongest between 11:00 AM and 3:00 PM. If this coincides with the event's hours, plan accordingly.

Find out what special activities they have for children guests ahead of time. This way you can plan what activities your children will participate in, and which ones you may choose to avoid. (yes, you have seen this advice before). If you ever had a "water baby" than you understand how difficult it can be to peel a child away from water activities. Thus, a water activity may be one you skip.

Don't assume your younger children will be able to participate in all the activities like the ones at Skyline Ranch. Activities may have age and height requirements. Also, you may see less than enthusiastic adult players when your child comes to join in the fun. If they do have competitive or challenging games for your littles, practice at home to reduce frustration if you can. Do some relay races, three-legged races, and practice taking turns so kids can learn the rules for the various activities. Next, create a calming strategy in advance with your child to help them avoid reacting like a sore loser.

Take a break from the activities. Take a time out from the activities, even if it means you retreat to your car. Some outdoor picnic venues offer air-conditioned pavilions, but in case your event doesn't, have a cool, quiet time in the car. You can't expect your kids to be at their best when they are overly hot and tired.If your company summer party is an all-day affair, **consider leaving early** or agree to stay for only a certain amount of time. My event sitting company provided care for an international company's annual summer party that took over a country club for the day and the ballroom in the evening. The club and company had worked together to provide swimming, tennis, and golf lessons, and a full menu of non-stop activities. With families not taking breaks, only a quarter of the children guests made it to the evening dinner, despite the wonderful accommodations that had been made for them.

Host tip:

When considering the date, work around school schedules. Plan the date for your spring or summer holiday party around your local school district's Spring Break, or right before summer break is over.

Ask employees what they want. When polling employees or forming committees who will oversee the spring/summer party, be sure to enlist employees with younger children. They will help everyone understand special accommodations for kids. For example, do you need two bounce houses, one for older kids and one for younger kids? For safety reasons it's typically not a good idea for younger and older kids to bounce together.

Planner tips:

Plan more for younger kids than just crayons and coloring books. Little kids will quickly get bored when they see all the other activities available for everyone else.

Consider activities for parents who are not able to get away from little ones (carriers and strollers). These activities might not be for kids exactly, but parents want to have fun without stressing about their little one. For example, you can plan a scavenger hunt and pair teams of "stroller/carrier" parents and people who aren't tethered. They would take a stroller-friendly route to find a list of items you know they will see at the event (even if they are things you have planted).

Set up barricades to prevent little people from interrupting games or activities that could be a danger to them. Or create a special area allocated to younger kids. Keep the littles out of the middle of jumbo beer pong.

Church

Church is a place of worship, learning lessons, and social gatherings. Many churches have established nurseries and children's ministries. For our purposes, we will address what to do if you are an invited guest to a church for a special service where nursey is not provided. Sometimes my event sitting company is contacted to provide nursery attendant services because their usual volunteers have been relieved to attend the service. But be aware that often the church might decide to just close the nursery.

Sitting in a crowded sanctuary with the *holy and sanctified* can be daunting with younger children who don't understand the civility of the environment.

Parent Preparation:

Be strategic about where you sit. If you can seat yourself, sit close to other families with young children. Folks with children will be more forgiving of little ones' sights, sounds, and smells. Also, your child will not be singled out if there are a number of littles to pin loud talk and noises to. If there aren't several families seated in a concentrated area, sit near the back so you can quickly exit the room if necessary.

Create a coloring clipboard. I must credit this ingenious idea to one of our church clients. Place blank coloring sheets on a clipboard. The clipboard provides a hard surface and is better than your Bible, hymnal, or pew. Also, this prevents several church programs from becoming makeshift coloring pages.

Church

Host/Planner tips:

Consider hiring an event sitting company who may have a sliding scale or non-profit rate. If you are expecting a lot of children, you can't hope and pray they will all behave.

Recruit volunteers outside of your church. Several American high schools have AVID, a college-readiness program designed to help students develop the skills they need to be successful in college. Typically, this program requires several community service hours. You could take advantage of school district community boards and school guidance counselors to advertise the opportunity.

Make a room available to parents. Parents will appreciate a space outside of the vestibule or restroom to calm their children or take a break.

Church

Weddings

The rest of the book will be dedicated to weddings. Remember how I mentioned in the beginning that my sister's wedding had event childcare? That was a solution to a large problem, which prompted me to start my event babysitting company, Black-Tie Babysitting Inc. My sister was getting married and decided she wanted a formal, adult-only affair. Well, to say this was difficult was an understatement. I am Nigerian American, and in our culture families are important, and children, welcomed or not, come to all events. I was very vocal about my distain for my sister's decision, and she challenged me to come up with a solution.

At the time, I employed a part-time nanny for my children. So I asked her if she and a few of her friends could watch the kids at my sister's wedding for a couple of hours. While on a venue tour, I remembered a room that we had access to which wasn't being used. We could use this room for the kids. Fast forward to the wedding day: I packed my kid's toys, put some hot dogs in a slow cooker, and made a makeshift check-in sheet. This is a far cry from our current digital check-in system, 200 square foot storage of toys and baby gear, and sitters across 4 states. It was sparse, but it worked.

After the reception, the parents raved about the service and demanded to know the name of the event babysitting company. So, without a business name, card, or plan, I claimed it. I told the parents to write down their email addresses and I would get information to them. I would like to say, I moved forward with my business the very next day. But it took three years before I had a true business. Now we have overseen more than 200 events, and have served close to 4,000 children guests. Weddings still make up 85% of our business, which is why half of this book is dedicated to weddings.

This section of the book is organized differently because it is devoted to one occasion. It still has tips for parents, but the advice is customized for the different roles they play from being a guest all the way up to being the couple getting married. There won't be host tips per say, but more tips for the professional planner. These suggestions are based on the assumption that there is no professional event childcare offered at the wedding.

There will be more stories in this section, because action leads to insight more often than insight leads to action.

Weddings

Parent Guest

Brides and grooms take painstaking steps to ensure that all their invited guest have an unforgettable experience at their wedding. Children guests can make a costly emotional and financial impact if not planned for. So go to the couple's wedding website to check if children guests are encouraged to attend. You may see a cute little phrase, "Leave the littles. We adore your children but have limited space (and intend to party). Please make it a date night." Translation: Get a babysitter. Another indicator can be found on the invitation and/or RSVP card. If this is your couple's decision, you need to respect it and not circumvent them.

I once had a wedding planner tell me about a group of parent guests who took it upon themselves to overturn the bride and groom's decision. The bride and groom both came from large families with lots of children, but made the hard decision not to invite kids because of the formalness of the wedding and their venue. The family was so surprised on the bride's side that they started contacting her mother. Unfortunately her mother then told everyone that there had been a mistake and the children were free to come! The bride caught wind of the situation and asked (paid) the planner to call each of the guests personally. The planner had to explain that indeed it was an adult only reception, and if they had not made proper arrangements for their kids, she would regrettably need to cancel their RSVP. Yikes!

If children are encouraged to come, get a tag team partner. Most weddings are family affairs, so if you find yourself solo, enlist the help of a grandparent, cousin, or friend who is attending. During the ceremony a loud child, even if only cooing, can be distracting. Sit close to the back, so that if your child needs to leave, your exit can be swift. I had a mother-of-the bride approach me at a bridal show after she figured out about my business. She told me a child guest had screamed through her entire ceremony 25 years prior, and she had never forgotten.

At the reception, if your child is struggling through the introductions and speeches, take them out too. This is where you can tag your partner, if you don't want to miss a special speech or the mother-groom-dance.

With this guide I have tried my best not to tell you *what not to do* but rather how to do things better. However, do not let your little one wonder around unescorted (even amongst family). There are hazards all around including centerpieces, décor, and sound and lighting equipment. In fact, a while ago there was a national story about a toddler tripping over a photographer's equipment. The toddler's fall resulted in a brain injury. Scan the room for "little people landmines." These are wedding extras that could cause your little one to explode if they can't have it or participate in it right away. Examples of these landmines include (but are not limited to) donut walls, candy/dessert tables, glow light stations, and photobooths. By scanning the reception, you can stay clear of them when you are socializing, making trips to the buffet, or visiting the bathroom with your little one.

If the meal is not plated, tag your partner. Take turns getting food. Typically, children in our care are served a separate buffet in our care room, but every blue moon we will have to walk with them through the buffet line. Little people cause congestion in buffet lines because they don't have a sense of urgency to get through it, and they want to negotiate what goes on their plate.

Weddings

The dance party is probably the most highly anticipated thing at a wedding, second only to the bride's dress. Try to hold your child off the dancefloor or to the side for the first 30 to 45 minutes of dancing after the dancefloor is opened. I had a DJ tell me that once littles get on the floor, the mood of the party shifts and it turns into a kid party.

Now, if you are a traveling parent-guest all the same tips apply, but I do have a few other things to add. Wedding weekends have become very popular. These include events hosted by the wedding couple, outside of the wedding—a rehearsal dinner or a brunch the day after. If you are invited to these events, I would suggest getting a guest-room sitter who can watch your kids at the hotel. Not only can you employ their services to cover these extra events, but the night of the wedding they could meet you back at the hotel for a quick drop-off and change (kids in pjs) so you can dance the night away. This way the children can still attend the wedding and see family and friends, but you get a semi-date night for a few hours.

Check with your hotel to see if they carry play-yards or cribs so you don't have to travel with baby gear in addition to your luggage. Note the hotel play-yards are typically the older style with no mattress. Even while providing care at a 4-star hotel, I have experienced poor quality baby sleeping solutions. If your hotel doesn't have play-yards/cribs, there are a handful of companies who rent baby gear for three days minimum and offer delivery and pick-up.

I don't believe in absolutes, so I will highlight one hotel group doing it right. At a cost of $1 million in 2001, Starwood hotels and resorts replaced all the cribs considered unsafe in its Westin and Sheraton Four Points hotels throughout North America. The hotels brought in the "Heavenly Crib" and the "Sweet Sleeper Crib" in response to the U.S. Consumer Product Safety

Commission and the National SAFE Kids campaign report that they had found unsafe cribs and play-yards in the majority of hotels they visited around the country. I will stress again, check with your hotel first. Don't get stuck with an unsafe crib, because you were caught unaware.

Weddings

Planner Tips

Creating a guest list can be challenging in and of itself, but this is a good time to sit with your couple and decide if their wedding will be a child-free event. If they decide they will welcome children guests, go back over the RSVPs with kids and follow up with them closer to the wedding. Some parents are adamantly against bringing children to formal affairs and your couple may be counting kids who are not even coming. Half the battle is knowing how many children will be there. In our experience, a wedding with 150 adult guests will have an additional 25 kids on average. Understand 25 kids is a lot at a wedding. Another way to look at it: the Texas Agency recommends a class size of 22 kids for pre-k classrooms. This limit is for a place that was imagined and created specifically for kids.

Seat your guests with children together when creating a seating chart. Guests with children will be more patient and forgiving of little guest's behavior. Also, guests with children may be more conscious of their own behavior including language and alcohol consumption. Aside from seating your child-friendly guests together, ask the venue if there is another room you can have as a "chill-down" area for tired children and nursing mothers.

Before special dances/speeches, ask the DJ to make an announcement. The announcement does not have to be rude, and can be generalized to everyone. Something like, "Please no moving around as the bride and groom approach the floor for their first dance."

Catered meals account for a good part of the wedding budget. If your client chooses to have a seated dinner, ask if the caterer provides children's plates. Children's plates are not normally the same price and reduce waste. If the couple has a buffet, see if a small section can be dedicated to children guest food options. Parents can make their children's plates quickly without congestion and negotiation in the adult buffet.

Advise your clients when they determine room blocks to include at least one hotel that is child-friendly with specific accommodations. A few of these accommodations may be hotels offering one, two, and three-bedroom suites, or hotels that have cribs, refrigerators and microwaves in the room upon request.

Weddings

Bridal Party Parent

Typically, no matter what time the wedding starts, being a bridesmaid or groomsman is an all-day affair. Not to mention the time commitment for the ceremony rehearsal and rehearsal dinner. Having to balance kids during this whirlwind of a schedule is tough. I suggest a private conversation with the bridal couple upon being asked to participate in the wedding. Help them understand how excited you are about their upcoming nuptials, and that you are flattered to be part of their special day. However, because of your younger kids, you will need the couple to work with you on certain aspects so you can still take full part in their day without sacrificing your responsibilities as a parent.

For example, ask the bride if you can be the last person to have your hair and make-up done, so you don't have to be available exactly when they start. You can reserve this time to be with your kids in the morning. If bridesmaids/groomsmen are helping with decorating the venue, ask if you can sit this out and help with things that need to be prepared before the wedding (like folding programs). Ask to help with things you can do from home or your hotel room, so you're not leaving your kids.

This may be hard to do, but ask the couple to help cover some of the expenses for a private sitter instead of giving you a bridesmaid or groomsmen gift. According to gift etiquette, these gifts should be 10–25% of the bridal parties' expenses. This won't pay for the service entirely but could help. Alternatively, you could ask if they could give you an additional plus one so you can

Weddings

bring someone who could help with your child at the wedding and other activities.

If you are a nursing bridesmaid and plan on breastfeeding, ask the planner if you can see the wedding day timeline. This will let you know when you must absolutely be around (i.e. group pictures, bridal party introductions, and speeches) and you can plan nursing breaks accordingly.

Being in several bridal & groom suites with my other business, a dress concierge and onsite steaming service, I noticed there is typically only one meal served the entire day to the bridal party before the wedding. Whether it be breakfast or lunch, just one meal. While you may be okay with this, make sure you remember to plan for your kids to eat. I have been with so many children who are hangry and irritable from food neglect. You can't expect your kids to be on their best behavior if they are hungry.

Planner Tip:

Try to tidy the bridal suite before everyone starts lining up (if onsite) or boards the bus to go to the ceremony. The suite may serve as a mothering room for a nursing bridesmaid that needs to feed her baby quickly in-between responsibilities.

Weddings

Mommy Bride/ Daddy Groom

The bride and groom should have a wonderful experience on their wedding day. It should be a time spent together celebrating this ultimate expression of love. But fortunately, or unfortunately, you cannot table your parent responsibilities during wedding planning or on your wedding day. However, you can reduce your stress, be the couple of honor, and share memorable moments with your children with the right preparation.

Like we stated earlier, your wedding is an all-day affair for your bridal party, but on average for marrying couples it has been a long 13 to 18 months. Black-Tie Babysitting does offer a Mommy Bride-to-Be package that takes care of your children during appointments with wedding vendors, dress fittings, and other pre-wedding activities. For more information check-out our website.

For the purpose of this book we will focus on your wedding day. Parent preparation is paramount, because more than likely your children will be with you intermittently, and you will rely on other people for child-minding. As an example of what can go right: we had a client couple who had two young children. They had their wedding at a ranch where the bridal party stayed onsite in the ranch bunk houses. The youngest child (2 years) was very attached to his mother. She hired our event sitting company for 14 hours of service. That morning she handed over her boys with a list of instructions and a stocked fridge. Also, she handed us both of their suits and shoes. She was nearby in the bridal suite enjoying brunch with her bridesmaids. We had a timeline of her day, so we knew what time the boys needed to be dressed, and where they needed to be for important moments. That was great planning on her part.

Whether your child will be getting ready with you or with somebody else, create a box for them. I suggest a 14.5-gallon storage bin that can be reused. This bin is large enough to store their shoes without taking them out of the shoe box, and store their outfit neatly folded in a garment bag. All their accessories like hairbows and socks can go in the bin as well. There is enough space for the diaper bag, special pillows, and blankets too. Plus it can be easily transported. The goal is to have everything packed so that nobody will bother you with questions like, "Where are the hair ties for your daughter?"

Be sure to plan your child's meals. I have been with several children who were in the bridal party who had styled hair, mini- manicures, adorable suits with the perfect bowtie, but were food neglected because nobody thought to feed them amid the list of to-dos.

Next, incorporate a special time with your child if you know they are not going to make it through the ceremony. Our bride arranged a pre-photo wedding shoot with just her boys in the bounce house they rented for the wedding. To see the pictures, visit our website. She decided, based on the behavior of her youngest at the rehearsal dinner, that he would not be able to sit through the ceremony. By planning this special time pre-wedding, she was able to create a moment that was equally as memorable as him being in the ceremony.

Have your child-minder take a fabric lunch sack to the reception. They can easily carry it to collect all the accessories littles tend to discard after a long day of being cute. This is easier than individually collecting cast-off bows and pacifiers, then returning to a seat to place each item in a diaper bag.

Weddings

Have a special meal of the children's favorite food if you are having a plated dinner. If they are concentrating on eating their favorite meal, they may not even notice you sitting at your table. If this is not possible, make sure they are seated with their child-minder where you are not in view. The little boy we watched was okay most of the reception, because he could not see his mother and father seated at their table.

If your child's grandparents or other recognizable family members plan on giving speeches, this may be a time for children to take a break from the reception. They will not care about the order of ceremony. They will just see Grandpa, and want to get his attention.

Be sure to have a plan for how to get your child home after the reception. I had a bride who was getting married at a luxury city club. The club did not provide kid's meals and the plated meal carried a hefty price tag of $80 per person. This wasn't a manageable price considering they had over 30 children guests RSVP plus four children of their own. Her planner contacted Black-Tie and we were able to watch the children at a neighboring hotel in a meeting room. The children enjoyed games, toys and pizza, which was probably more appealing to their pallet. At the end of the evening all the children had been picked up except for the bride and groom's kids. After numerous texts with the planner, the kids were picked up 45 minutes later by their grandparents, who were flagged down as they were about to get into their car to leave. I shudder at the thought of needing to call the bride and groom on their wedding night to come pick up their kids. (Don't let this happen to you.)

Also make sure your pickup arrangements are realistic. I had a couple who already had a home together where they were raising a blended family with kids and the bride's mother. The bride happened to be one of my sitters and a neighbor. Black-Tie provided services during her ceremony, but I attended as a guest and steamed her bridal parties' apparel. When her mother arrived for hair and makeup, I greeted her and a carload of stuff. I helped with unloading, but she still looked anxious. When I asked her what was wrong, she told me the couple was expecting her to bring everything back to their home after the wedding—including their 6 kids! I assured her my husband and I would help. After everything was said and done, it took three SUV's to bring all the stuff and the children home. Thankfully, the bride is a great person with friends who rallied together to help.

Planner Tips:

If your couple has children, implore them to hire a professional event sitter, nanny, or childcare professional. Weddings are family affairs. Grandparents, cousins, uncles, and aunties all have a vested interested in being involved in the wedding and will be too be distracted to give younger children the attention they need.

Additionally, do not put this responsibility on church nursery workers at $10 per hour. To child-mind in a restricted environment for a few hours on Sunday morning does not prepare them for an intense 10 to 14-hour wedding day. Likewise avoid sitters listed on the various babysitting/nanny websites. These sitters are not contractually obligated and may not show up (we tried in the past to supplement our staff with people from these sites and they were no- shows). I had a bride tell me she hired a sitter off Care.com. The sitter said she would be able to bring a friend if they could use the extra help. The bride agreed and both girls showed up. The friend did not help with the kids, but socialized as if she was an invited guest and left early. The other sitter stayed the duration of the wedding then called her ride. Her ride never showed up and she could not get anyone else to come pick her up. The wedding took place at a secluded ranch in Oklahoma. The sitter ended up having to stay in the bride and groom's cabin on their wedding night because there was no other room available. The sitter was finally picked up the following morning. When you hire a professional, there is a firewall consisting of contracts, reputation, and brand that would not allow a situation like this to occur.

Weddings

If the child is part of the wedding and looks like they will not be able to make it through the ceremony, create an exit plan for them after they walk or are pulled down the aisle. We did an ultra-luxury modern wedding with glass and flowers elegantly decorating the ceremony space (not exactly child-friendly). The bride had 5 younger kids in her party. Literally they walked down the aisle then continued out a door and down a hall where we were waiting to take them to the care room until it was time for group pictures.

Be sure to provide the child-minder with the complete timeline so they know when the child must be present. There may be times the child needs a nap or a break. Make sure the child-minder can plan accordingly.

Help your couple understand how hard you have worked to create an experience they will be proud of, and that their children can't have full reign of all the extras (i.e. dessert table, photobooth, or glow light station). Your vendors will thank you if you make this clear up front.

Be sure to include the child's comings and goings in the timeline like pickup details.

Weddings

To Be Continued...

Well, I guess if this were a children's story book it would say, "The End." But this isn't the end. This is just what I want to say as of right now. Hopefully, I haven't overwhelmed or underwhelmed you at this point. There will always be more to write about as new party and wedding trends play a very important role in how my event sitting company prepares for our clients. I hope this book helps parents say yes to parties first, before assuming that having kids is the reason they should say "no." Additionally I hope this book has given some insight to planners and hosts. I would love to get reader feedback with savvy tips and stories that we can use in future editions. Tag your successful partying pictures on social media with our hashtag #YesWithKids.

I appreciate you reading this book and want to help you in any way I can. If you have questions about this book and want to chat, visit our company website and the book landing page.

To Be Continued...

Appendices

Special Needs Children

Xavier is my awesome autistic son. He was diagnosed at the age of 4. After sharing with my father Xavier's diagnosis, my father asked, "how do we cure him." I explained to him that Xavier didn't have an illness but a viewpoint of the world that was different from others, but was equally important and equally necessary.

In school there are accommodations, but in the outside world it's the parents of special needs children that act as a buffer and modify situations so that the children can be comfortable (not to be confused with making other people comfortable with our children). While I do have advice to offer, I caution forcing your children to attend events that just don't make sense for them.

I remember making this mistake. Our city was hosting animatronic dinosaurs. Thousands of parents (myself included) and children paid to see elaborate vignettes and life-size dinosaurs—what kid wouldn't love this experience? My son didn't like standing in line, the crowds and the exhibits were too much. After paying $80 for entrance fees, we left within 5 minutes. After learning from this experience, we didn't go to see Santa at the mall or do several other things seen as necessary for conventional childhood. We created new experiences and traditions.

I know special occasions and family events are not as easy to close the door on. So I created the helper acronym N.E.E.D to help parents of special needs children qualify events, and prepare appropriately when they do attend.

N.E.E.D.

"N" is for *next time*.

Does your child *need* to go? Will there be another opportunity for your child to attend the event in a different setting (maybe more intimate) or when they have the coping skills to better handle the uncertainty of the event details (i.e. sounds and smells). Today, my son could easily attend an event where he would have to wait in line. However, he would ask several times

Appendices

when we would be able to go in and he needs to hold Legos while we wait.

"E" is for encounter.

What things could your child encounter that could cause them to be uncomfortable or distressed? Consider both intangible and tangible things and determine potential fixes. If you know the event will be loud, then you might want to have your child use noise cancellation headphones. If your child has a sensitivity to smell, soak a handkerchief in a calming scent. Your child can hold it to their nose if there is a discomforting smell. Check with the event organizer to see if these stressors will be part of the event. I once had a child in my care who was terrified of balloons. We had balloon volleyball activity planned for an event. When I saw the child's terror as we began to hand out the balloons, I immediately ended everything, but I had to deal with the disappointed children who had their balloons taken back. If I had prior knowledge of this fear, we wouldn't have even attempted the activity.

"E" is for enjoy or endure.

Will your child enjoy the event or endure it? In the previous example of my dinosaur excursion, I believed my son should have *enjoyed it,* but didn't think about him just enduring it. Honestly, I have seen special needs kids at events in corners with tablets, but they are invisible to the event. I would encourage parents to find a way to help their child enjoy the event. At a wedding you could request a song you know they will love to dance to or give them a piece of cake you know they will relish. If they love to draw, have them create a drawing to give the couple getting married beforehand or during the reception. Also, check to see if your local

Appendices

event and wedding professional childcare provider has a service for special needs kids. Black-Tie has a suite of special needs services including de-escalation kits with peaceful playdough and coloring books. Also, we offer a sitter who can individually shadow special needs children so they can enjoy the evening however they feel most comfortable. For example, my son, Xavier, loves to pace and uses scripted language to calm himself in new situations. His behavior may seem disruptive during a speech or special moment during the reception, so one of our shadows would help him get to a hallway where he could be himself without disrupting. You can also create a social story ahead of time—a short story that describes a social situation your special needs child may encounter. In the story, the event details are outlined, making it recognizable and easier for your child to relate when the actual situations occur. The story has instructions on how your child should respond in the specific situation. These social stories can be a great way for your family to get involved. You can use actual pictures of people or ask siblings to help illustrate.

"D" is for determine.

You ultimately must make the decision if your special needs child should attend the event, and under what circumstances you will stay or leave. It takes discipline to follow the formula, but failing to do so may carry high cost for you and your child. We had some parents drop their child off in event care without letting us know they had special needs. We give parents the opportunity to do this discreetly, *but I knew*. Their child would not go to the bathroom with our sitters and ended up making a mess on himself. We had to get his parents out of the event, because they didn't provide us a change of clothes. To my amazement, they chose to not leave the event, and changed their son into his younger brother's pull-ups (with no pants), then returned to the party. He

Appendices

was about 7-years-old. At this point, the other children wouldn't play with him.

I care about the health and safety of you and your children. I am always open to brainstorm with parents to figure out how to prepare their special needs child for events, but it's important to be open and honest about what your child needs.

ChangerClutch

www.changerclutch.com

Although the word essential will never be the same post COVID-19, the Changer Clutch is described as the essential piece for every new mother's closet. It has a waterproof changing mat and a large pocket that can hold all your things too.

Appendices

Controlling Anger Technique

Teaching children how to control anger on impulse is a useful skill for when children will be playing games or interacting closely with others.

While we want to believe our authoritative command to tell our child to calm down will be enough to get our kids past a tantrum, it's highly likely it won't be. I came across a great technique that educators use for cognitive behavioral intervention. The "turtle technique" has been used successfully with preschool and kindergarten age children for years. The basic steps of the turtle technique are: 1) recognizing that you feel angry, 2) thinking to "stop," 3) going into your "shell" and taking three deep breaths an thinking calming, coping thoughts. You can practice the turtle technique with role play or discussing previous incidents when your child was not a good sport.

Practice this technique before you attend events that are competitive or may require your child to use patience. To remind them get a turtle sticker you can place on their hand as a gentle reminder. Or give them a small plastic turtle to hold. The turtle could help your child recall the steps to keep calm and think of solutions if they feel they are losing control.

Appendices

Acknowledgements

I would like to thank:

God for being forever faithful. I can't even walk without holding his hand, much less write a book.

Stephen & Theresa Oriabure (my parents). By their faith they named me Hope, and by their faithfulness I have survived. I know it wasn't always easy to love me, but they did.

Stephannie (Ebhota), James, and Shenna. These are my siblings who at times seemed impossible, but they are so amazing and have inspired me by their own journeys to success.

Jalen, Harmony, Xavier, and Zachary (my children). You all are my life. You all have fueled my desire to be the best version of myself so I could raise you to be at your best.

Fatesta Bateman and Shae Roundtree my dearest friends. You have always been a shoulder for me to cry on, have been a sounding board, and never failed to give me the truth even if I didn't want to accept it.

Mrs. Wentz my fourth-grade teacher, who raved about a story I wrote and planted the seed that I could be a writer.

About the Author

e Oriabure Hunter, but you can call me Mommy Deluxe.

(Did you have a Barbie Deluxe Camper growing up? You know, the one with the bed, kitchen, camping gear and a pool? It was one of my favorite toys.)

Just like Barbie's camper, I have all the bells and whistles:

I'm a mom of four, a wife, and a devoted daughter.

I love talkin' politics, dancin' to Afrobeats and cookin' up a storm.

I went to college, went to work in the corporate world, and now I'm a busy entrepreneur.

I'm so much more than just a mom, but when my kids were little, it was really hard for me to embrace the "deluxe" part of my life. I am now on a mission to help other mothers know it's okay to want more than to be a Mommy.

About Black-Tie Babysitting

Black-Tie Babysitting provides onsite childcare at special occasions and weddings. We specialize in weddings, conventions, family reunions, and any other large event that might not otherwise be for kids. We bring our sitters to the event location to entertain and supervise the children so adult guests can relax and enjoy themselves.

We are an elevated babysitting service with a carefully curated experience including engaging sitters, toys, custom crafts, and tailored activities. Becausue no parent should have to stay home just because they can't find childcare.

Headquarters in Dallas, TX. We serve North Texas & DMV areas.

Contact us for more information:

214-450-1245

info@blacktiebabysitting.com

Website: www.blacktiebabysitting.com

IG: @blacktiebabysitting

FB: https://www.facebook.com/specialeventsitter/

BLACK-TIE
Babysitting

Rolling out the red carpet for your littlest gues